I0559082

# AIN'T NO
# SHAME

This journal belongs to:

_____

Ain't No Shame: Embrace the Past, Accept the Present, and Move On To The Future Workbook

Copyright © 2024 by Treisha Parker Combo

ISBN: 979-8-9914673-0-8

Published by: Open Door Publishing, LLC.
Printed in the United States of America

Internal Layout and Design: InSCRIBEd Inspiration, LLC.
Edited by:          Penda L. James, and
                    Treisha Parker-Combo

Cover Art: Photo by Annie Spratt on Unsplash
Cover Design: InSCRIBEd Inspiration
Author Photos:  HD Visuals, Hannah Davis

All real-life anecdotes are told with permission from actual parties involved and recorded to the best of the author's recollection. Names in some instances have not been used at the request of the individuals referenced. In some cases, parties mentioned are deceased. Details of some instances have been slightly modified to enhance readability, or to ensure privacy. Any resemblance of any other parties is purely coincidental.

All rights reserved. No part of this book may be reproduced or transmitted in any form electronic, or mechanical, including photocopying and recording, or held in any information storage and retrieval system without permission in writing from the author and publisher.

Scriptures taken from the Holy Bible, New International Version®, NIV®. Copyright © 1973, 1978, 1984, 2011 by Biblica, Inc.™ Used by permission of Zondervan. All rights reserved worldwide. www.zondervan.com The "NIV" and "New International Version" are trademarks registered in the United States Patent and Trademark Office by Biblica, Inc.®

# DEDICATION

*For women who have experienced shame and trauma,*
*you can come out of it unbound and free.*

Love,
Treisha

*The fear of the Lord is the beginning of wisdom; all who follow his precepts have good understanding.*

~Psalm 111:10

# HOW TO USE THIS WORKBOOK/JOURNAL

This book is for people who have been through something that caused them to feel ashamed, and they have a hard time overcoming it. I am the voice that will not keep silent to help you break free from shame.

There are questions in this workbook. You can use them with my book, Aint' No Shame: Embrace The Past, Accept The Present, and Move On To The Future, or alone. These are conversation starters that will help you as an individual, or your group reflect and gather gems to overcome shame and lean on God.

### Get Started

You don't have to wait to get to your healing. Pray and ask God to guide you. Pull out your phone, look at your calendar and schedule time to work on yourself. Set reminders in case you forget. Take 30 minutes or an hour every day to reflect on a question and write your answers. Once you have reflected, implement your action plan to help you get moving again.

# IDEAS TO HELP YOU GET STARTED:

1. Meet with your pastor or spiritual leader to get guidance on your next steps.
2. Find an accountability partner who will hold you accountable to achieve your goals. Ask them to check on you to make sure you are being productive.
3. Surround yourself with people who are doing what you want to do already so you can learn and see what they are doing.
4. Don't be afraid to pivot or move on from situations and people that are holding you back from getting to your destiny.
5. Make sure that you are healthy in mind, body and spirit. Exercise, drink water, take deep breaths and keep God First.

#  MEDITATION SCRIPTURES

*Cast all your cares on the Lord.*

I Peter 5:7

*Favor is deceitful and beauty is vain but a woman that fears the Lord she shall be praised.*

Proverbs 31:30

*For the Scripture says, 'Whoever believes in Him will not be put to shame.*

Romans 10:11

*If we confess our sins, He is faithful and just to forgive us our sins and to cleanse us from all unrighteousness.*

1 John 1:9

*Give thanks to the God of heaven. His love endures forever.*

Psalm 136:26 (NIV)

*Do not be anxious about anything, but in every situation, by prayer and petition, with thanksgiving, present your requests to God.*

Philippians 4:6 (NIV)

*Now faith is confidence in what we hope for and assurance about what we do not see.*

Hebrews 11:1 (NIV)

*Commit thy way unto the Lord; trust also in him; and he shall bring it to pass.*

Psalm 37:5

*Trust in the Lord with all thine heart; and lean not unto thine own understanding. In all thy ways acknowledge him, and he shall direct thy paths.*

Proverbs 3:5-6

★ My favorite scriptures that helped me overcome shame . . .

_____

_____

_____

_____

_____

_____

_____

_____

_____

_____

_____

_____

_____

_____

★ How can I be more aligned with God?

_____

_____

_____

_____

_____

_____

_____

_____

_____

_____

_____

_____

_____

_____

_____

★ I describe my faith as . . .

_____

_____

_____

_____

_____

_____

_____

_____

_____

_____

_____

_____

_____

_____

_____

★ How do I let my light shine?

_____

_____

_____

_____

_____

_____

_____

_____

_____

_____

_____

_____

_____

_____

_____

_____

_____

_____

*For there is nothing hidden
that will not be disclosed,
and nothing concealed
that will not be known
or brought out into the open.*

*Luke 8:17*

★ Sacrifices I can make to overcome shame. . .

_____

_____

_____

_____

_____

_____

_____

_____

_____

_____

_____

_____

_____

_____

_____

_____

_____

_____

_____

_____

_____

_____

_____

_____

_____

_____

_____

_____

_____

_____

_____

_____

_____

_____

★ A pivotal moment for me. . .

_____

_____

_____

_____

_____

_____

_____

_____

_____

_____

_____

_____

_____

_____

_____

_____

★ How can I move on from shame?

_____

_____

_____

_____

_____

_____

_____

_____

_____

_____

_____

_____

_____

_____

_____

_____

★ I see myself. . . .

_____

_____

_____

_____

_____

_____

_____

_____

_____

_____

_____

_____

_____

_____

_____

_____

_____

★ Loving myself looks like. . .

_____

_____

_____

_____

_____

_____

_____

_____

_____

_____

_____

_____

_____

_____

_____

★ Is there someone or something holding me back from being my best?

_____

_____

_____

_____

_____

_____

_____

_____

_____

_____

_____

_____

_____

_____

_____

_____

**AIN'T NO**
*SHAME*

★ Who are the people I can count on?

_____

_____

_____

_____

_____

_____

_____

_____

_____

_____

_____

_____

_____

_____

_____

_____

★ What are the resources I have surrounded myself with?

_____

_____

_____

_____

_____

_____

_____

_____

_____

_____

_____

_____

_____

_____

★ How do I want to grow?

_____

_____

_____

_____

_____

_____

_____

_____

_____

_____

_____

_____

_____

_____

_____

★ What am I going to do about my peace?

_____

_____

_____

_____

_____

_____

_____

_____

_____

_____

_____

_____

_____

_____

_____

_____

★ These are the steps I have taken (or plan to take) to reclaim my peace of mind . . .

_____

_____

_____

_____

_____

_____

_____

_____

_____

_____

_____

_____

_____

_____

_____

_____

**AIN'T NO**
*SHAME*

★ What do I say to myself about myself?

_____

_____

_____

_____

_____

_____

_____

_____

_____

_____

_____

_____

_____

_____

_____

_____

_____

_____

_____

_____

_____

_____

_____

_____

_____

_____

_____

_____

_____

_____

_____

# SETTING GOALS

Goal 1: 

Deadline:_____

Accountability Partner
_____

Action Steps
1.  _____
    _____
2.  _____
    _____
3.  _____
    _____

Goal 2: 

Deadline:_____

Accountability Partner
_____

Action Steps
1.  _____
    _____
2.  _____
    _____
3.  _____
    _____

Goal 3: 

Deadline:_____

Accountability Partner
_____

Action Steps
1.  _____
    _____
2.  _____
    _____
3.  _____
    _____

# SETTING GOALS

Goal 4: 

Deadline:_____

Accountability Partner

_____

Action Steps
1.  _____
    _____
2.  _____
    _____
3.  _____
    _____

Goal 5: 

Deadline:_____

Accountability Partner

_____

Action Steps
1.  _____
    _____
2.  _____
    _____
3.  _____
    _____

Goal 6: 

Deadline:_____

Accountability Partner

_____

Action Steps
1.  _____
    _____
2.  _____
    _____
3.  _____
    _____

★ What am I going to do about my happiness?

_____

_____

_____

_____

_____

_____

_____

_____

_____

_____

_____

_____

_____

**AIN'T NO** *SHAME*

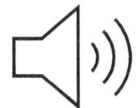

# AIN'T NO SHAME PLAYLIST

- "Feel Alright" Erica Campbell
- "Go Get It" Mary Mary
- "Goodness of God" CeCe Winans
- "Hang On" GEI
- "He's Able" Darwin Hobbs & Dietrich Haddon
- "Hold On" Sounds of Blackness
- "I Rely" Semaje
- "In spite of Me" Tasha Cobbs-Leonard
- "It's Gone Be Alright" Tye Tribbett
- "Jireh" Maverick City Music
- "Manifestation" Jakalyn Carr
- "Open Door Season" Deitrick Haddon
- "Optimistic" Sounds of Blackness
- "The Battle" Yolanda Adams
- "This Week" Anthony Brown and Group Therapy
- "When I Pray" Doe
- "Miracles" Kierra Sheard
- "Thank You Lord" Mary Mary
- "You Know my Name" Tasha Cobbs Leonard
- "I Just Wanna Praise You" Maurette Brown Clark

★ Songs I would recommend to others to help them overcome shame . . .

_____

_____

_____

_____

_____

_____

_____

_____

_____

_____

_____

_____

_____

_____

_____

*Instead of your shame
you will receive
a double portion,
and instead of disgrace
you will rejoice in your
inheritance.*

Isaiah 61:7 (NIV)

www.ingramcontent.com/pod-product-compliance
Lightning Source LLC
Chambersburg PA
CBHW051241120626
46547CB00014B/1736